# Jolly Good Cookin'

# Jolly Good Cookin!

Katelyn Jolly

Published by Katelyn Jolly, 2023.

While every precaution has been taken in the preparation of this book, the publisher assumes no responsibility for errors or omissions, or for damages resulting from the use of the information contained herein.

JOLLY GOOD COOKIN!

**First edition. November 24, 2023.**

Copyright © 2023 Katelyn Jolly.

ISBN: 979-8223406334

Written by Katelyn Jolly.

# Table of Contents

First of all this is for all my fellow foodies all over the world! Next, this is for my mom Susan and my better half and love, Greg. They both put up with me and my social media life and tell me when things are nasty! Dont worry! everything in here is from their approval! And finally nbcvxvbmnbv this is for my Bestie, Missy! With out her i wouldnt have anyone to panic to and say HELP! She always has some of the best advice! Keep an eye open for the ones by her!

THANK YOU EVERYONE! I LOVE YOU ALL!!!!

# Pot pie

INGREDIENTS

- 1 box store bought pie crust or 1 recipe for a 9" double crust pie
- 2 cups or 1 full chicken cooked and shredded
- 1 can each:
    A. Corn
    B. Carrots
    C. Peas
    D. Cream of chicken
    E. Cheddar cheese soup
- ½ cup milk

Directions

1. Preheat oven to 400 degrees F or 200 degrees C. Spray pie pan with cooking spray of choice. Roll out 1 crust and stretch over pie pan and gently push the crust down into the shape of the pan until it stays. Poke holes all over with a fork.
2. In a skillet heat shredded chicken with both cans of soup and milk. Mix until well blended. Then drain and

rinse all the cans of veggies and add to pan. Mix until heated through.

3.  Pour into pie crust and cover with the second crust. Pinch to close and seal with fork around edges.
4.  Poke holes or cut slits into top crust, brush with melted butter or egg wash and bake for 45 min to an hour depending on how thick your pie is!

If you want good gravy:

1 can cream of chicken

½ can water or more depending on thickness/thinness

To taste: (I start with about 1 teaspoon of each) rosemary, cilantro, salt, pepper, chives, minced garlic, parsley, and basil

Heat in small saucepan till it is as thin as you would like. I only do the half can, so it has some thickness to it! It will bubble when it is hot enough! Serve over cut pie pieces!

# Potato Chip Chicken

INGREDIENTS

- 2-3 medium to large cooked and shredded chicken breasts
- 1 cup mayonnaise
- 1 cup sour cream
- 1 can cream of chicken
- 1 can cheddar cheese soup
- 2 cups instant white rice cooked according to the box directions
- ¼ to ½ cup slivered almonds
- 2-4 cups cheese of choice (I use mozzarella and cheddar)
- Enough crushed chips to cover the top
  - I use either: Ruffles cheddar and sour cream, Ruffles sour cream and chives or plain wavy

Directions

1. Preheat oven to 350 degrees F or 175 degrees C
2. In a skillet, on medium-high heat, combine shredded chicken and both cans of soup, mix till smooth.

3.  Add both the mayonnaise and the sour cream, mix till smooth and then simmer on medium-low heat for about 5 minutes
4.  In another saucepan cook instant rice according to package. Once it's done add it to the chicken mixture and then add in almonds. Simmer for 5 minutes.
5.  In a greased 9X13 pan layer half chicken mix on the bottom. Add shredded cheese to cover the chicken mix. Then add remaining chicken mix
6.  Crush chips of choice and spread over top evenly! You can leave a few medium whole chips if you would like for decoration!
7.  Bake uncovered for 15-20 min! Or until it is bubbly!

# Queso-Ladda Bake

## INGREDIENTS

- 3 pounds ground beef
- 1 tablespoon minced garlic
- 1 tablespoon minced onion
- 1 15 oz can tomato sauce
- 1 ½ teaspoon cumin
- 1 teaspoon chili powder
- 1 teaspoon cilantro
- 2 cups salsa
- 6 soft taco shells split in half
- 6 cups shredded cheese
    - 3 cups fiesta
    - 3 cups mozzarella

## Directions

1. Preheat oven to 350 degrees F or 175 degrees C
2. Brown ground beef in a large skillet, over high heat. Drain and return to heat
3. Stir in the next 7 ingredients. Bring to a simmer and reduce to medium-low heat and simmer for 15

minutes

4. In a greased 9X13 pan spread half of the meat mix on the bottom of the pan and then cover with 3 tortillas split in half. Place the flat side of the tortillas to the pan walls, 1 for each end and 2 for the side walls!
5. Cover with 4 cups of shredded cheese, 2 fiesta and 2 mozzarella
6. Place remaining shells on top in same pattern.
7. Sprinkle remaining meat mix on top and spread evenly. Cover tightly with foil
8. Bake for 20 minutes then remove foil and sprinkle the last 2 cups of cheese over top and bake for an additional 10 minutes or until the cheese is bubbly!
9. Let cool for 5 minutes before cutting so it doesn't run everywhere!

# Taco Lasagna

HAVE PATIENCE, THIS is going to be like real lasagna with lots of layers!

Ingredients

- 3 pounds ground beef

- 2 packages taco seasoning
- 4 cloves minced or 1 tablespoon minced garlic
- ½ teaspoon cayenne pepper
- 1 tablespoon chili powder
- 1 ½ cup water
- 24 small corn tortillas
- 1 jar (24 oz) salsa
- 1 can chilies and diced tomatoes
- 1 16 oz container sour cream
- 4 cups shredded cheese: 2 cups fiesta 2 cups mozzarella

Directions

1. Brown and drain ground beef in a large deep skillet. Season with taco seasoning, garlic, cayenne pepper, chili powder, and water. Mix well and simmer for

10-12 minutes.

2. Meanwhile, preheat oven to 375 degrees F or 190 degrees C and grease 9X13 pan.
3. Layers:
    1. 6 Tortillas
    2. Spread 1/3 the salsa on top
    3. Spread 1/3 meat mix evenly
    4. Sprinkle with 1/3 can diced chilies and tomatoes
    5. Spread 1/3 sour cream on top
    6. Top with 1 cup cheese of choice, changing each layer
    7. Repeat this 2 more times for a total of 3 layers.
    8. Top layer is tortillas, salsa, and cheese sprinkled on top
4. Bake for 45 minutes or until cheese is melted and bubbly!

# Nacho Taco Bake

INGREDIENTS

- 3 pounds ground beef
- 1 can diced tomatoes and chilies
- 1 cup water
- 2 cup sour cream
- 2 packets taco seasoning
- 3 cups shredded fiesta/taco flavor cheese
- 1 bag taco chips

Directions

1. Preheat oven to 350 degrees F or 175 degrees C
2. In a large skillet, over medium-high heat, brown the ground beef then drain the grease
3. Add the next 4 ingredients, and let simmer for 10 minutes
4. In the bottom of a greased 9X13 pan place a layer of chips evenly
5. Next add 1/3 of the meat mix
6. 1 cup cheese on top
7. Repeat layers 2 more times. You might have taco chips

left which is fine! You can serve them with the bake!
8.  Bake for 20-25 minutes or until bubbly!

# Jolly Good Loose Meat

THESE ARE KNOWN IN the Midwest as Maid Rites, or just as loose meat sandwiches!

- 3 pounds ground beef
- 2 ½ tablespoon soy sauce
- 2 ½ tablespoon Worcestershire sauce (wash-your-sister sauce)
- 6 chicken bouillon cubes
- 6 beef bouillon cubes
- 2 ½ tablespoon brown sugar
- 2 ½ tablespoon apple cider vinegar
- 3 ½ tablespoons chopped onion

This can either be done in the crock pot on low for 6 hours or on the stove for 40 min total!

Crockpot: add ground beef and mash till separated. Then add all the rest, set your crockpot to low for 6 hours. You might want to stir once or twice while cooking!

Stovetop: brown ground beef in a Dutch oven on medium heat with all the bouillon cubes. Once the meat is brown (DO NOT DRAIN!!!) add in all the rest stir and turn down to low heat and simmer for 30-35 minutes!

*Serve these with buns or bread and your favorite condiments like ketchup and mustard!

# Weeknight Philly's

THIS ONE IS FROM MISSY! I call these my "bestie"-ipes

Ingredients

- 1-2 containers Shaved beef (we use the stuff from Aldi, it's so delicious!)
- 1 white onion
- 1 red pepper
- 1 green pepper
- 1 tablespoon oil for the skillet
- 1 tablespoon each: Cookies brand seasoning, lemon pepper seasoning, garlic powder, and onion powder
- 2 tablespoons "wash-your-sister" sauce (Worcestershire)
- 1 jar cheese whiz or Rico's liquid cheese
- Sliced cheese like provolone if you don't do liquid cheese
- 1 can mushrooms (optional)

Directions

1. Chop onion and peppers and toss into skillet over medium-high heat with oil and sauté till fragrant

2. Add shaved beef and season with all seasonings plus Worcestershire sauce, heat till meat is all one color!
3. Meanwhile, if using mushrooms, drop into small skillet and season with butter 1 teaspoon garlic powder and onion powder
4. Toast buns if you'd like! Melt cheese according to jar or can!
5. Make them however you want with your toppings!

# Corndog Bake

INGREDIENTS

- 12 Nathans brand hotdogs cut into small (but not too small!) pieces or what ever kind you like best
- 2 tablespoons oil to cook the hotdog pieces
- 2 large eggs
- 2 boxes Jiffy cornbread mix of whatever brand you like best
- 1 ½ cup 2% milk
- 2 teaspoons rubbed sage
- 3 cups shredded cheddar cheese
- Honey (optional)

Directions

1. Preheat oven to 400 degrees F or 200 C
2. In a medium skillet heat oil and add hotdog pieces. Sautee until tender and cooked through. Add any seasonings you'd like to at this time, but not necessary
3. Meanwhile, in a large bowl mix together the eggs, milk, sage, and honey. Add in the 2 boxes jiff and mix well.
4. Once the hotdog pieces cool a little, add them to the

cornbread mix. Stir to combine

5. Finally add in 2 cups of cheese, reserving 1 for the top!
6. Pour into a greased 9X13, drizzle with honey, then top with remaining cup of cheese and bake uncovered for 30-35 minutes!

# Turkey Dinner Leftover Surprise

DON'T KNOW WHAT TO do with all those holiday leftovers? Neither did I until I figured this one out! The more you have, the bigger (and better) this will be!

Ingredients

- 3 cups cooked stuffing
- 4 cups turkey, shredded
- ¾ cup mayonnaise, divided to ¼ cup and ½ cup
- ¼ cup cranberry sauce
- 2 cups mashed potatoes
- 2 cups shredded mozzarella

Directions

1. Preheat oven to 350 degrees F or 175 degrees C and grease a 9x13 baking dish
2. Cover bottom of dish with 1 ½ cups of stuffing then all of the turkey
3. Combine ¼ cup mayo with the cranberry sauce; spread over the turkey
4. Combine the ½ cup of the mayo with the mashed potatoes and cheese in a large bowl then spread evenly

over the cranberry layer

5. Cover with the remaining stuffing. Sprinkle cheese on top if you want
6. Bake in the oven for 40 minutes or until heated through. Let it stand for 5 minutes before serving
7. Serve with leftover gravy if you have any and any other leftovers you may have!

# Lasagna Toss

INGREDIENTS

- 3 pounds ground beef
- ½ cup chopped onion
- 5 large garlic cloves, minced
- 3 tablespoons Italian seasoning
- 1 12-ounce jar spaghetti sauce of choice!
- 6 ounces dry noodle of choice, cooked and drained
- 1 small tub cottage cheese
- 3 cups shredded mozzarella

Directions

1. Preheat oven to 350 degrees F or 175 degrees C
2. In a large skillet over medium-high heat, brown the ground beef and drain the grease. Add in onion, garlic, and seasonings. Mix till fragrant
3. Boil noodles according to package, drain and set aside
4. Stir in pasta sauce to the meat and simmer for 10 minutes. Stir in noodles
5. Spread half the meat mix on the bottom of a greased 9X13 pan.

6.  Spread cottage cheese evenly over the meat. Sprinkle with 2 cups of the cheese
7.  Pour the rest of the meat mix on top and sprinkle last cup of cheese on top
8.  Cover and bake for 20 minutes, remove, and bake for another 10.
9.  Let rest for 5 minutes before serving

# Chicken and Noodle

INGREDIENTS

- 1 full chicken (no more than a 5-pound bird)
- 1 24-ounce bag of egg noodles or homemade if you choose
- Seasonings of choice; I use about 2 tablespoons of salt, pepper, garlic powder and onion powder
- 1 stick of butter

Directions

1. Boil chicken with everything except the noodles for about 4 hours on medium-low heat
2. Once chicken starts to fall apart, remove chicken, and set broth to the side
3. Let the chicken cool so it's easier to shred! You don't want burnt fingers!
4. Once you start deboning the chicken, discard all the bones (break the wish bone and make a wish!) and all the skin!

5. When finished deboning the chicken and shredding it, toss it into the stock pot with the broth!
6. Set on medium-high heat and add noodles.
7. Simmer for about 15 minutes or until the egg noodles are tender!

We serve ours over mashed potatoes and have bread and crackers on the side!

# Meatloaf (Standard or Mini)

INGREDIENTS

- 2-3 pounds of ground beef thawed and pliable!
- 2 cups ketchup
- ½ cup salsa
- 1/8 cup yellow mustard
- 3 tablespoons wash-your-sister sauce (Worcestershire sauce)
- 1 tablespoon each:
    A. Garlic powder
    B. Onion powder
    C. Parsley
    D. Salt
    E. Pepper
    F. Cumin (optional)
- Use 2 sleeves of crackers for 3 pounds meat, 1 ½ sleeves for 2 pounds
- 2 eggs, beaten
- ¼ cup milk

Glaze

- 2/3 cup ketchup
- ¼ cup syrup
- Dash mustard powder
- Mix together and chill

Directions

1. Preheat oven to 375 degrees
2. Mix the first 5 ingredients together.
3. Add in the seasonings and mix together
4. Add the crackers milk and egg and mix till nice and blended
5. 1 whole loaf-
    a. Spray 9X13 pan and plop meat mix into the dish and spread out and flatten.
    b. Bake in the oven for 45 minutes till the last 10 min of bake time, take out and brush the glaze generously over the loaf and continue to bake for 10 more minutes
6. Minis-
    a. Split you mix into enough chunks for your mini meat loaf pan. I have 2 that I use, and they both have 8 spots
    b. Bake in the oven for 30-40 minutes till the last 10 min of bake time, take out and brush the glaze generously over the loaves and continue to bake for 10 more minutes
7. Remove from oven and let stand for 5 minutes before serving!

# Mac & Cheese

INGREDIENTS

- 1lb box noodles of choice!
- ½ brick of Velveeta cheese
- ½ cup milk or as needed
- ½ stick of salted butter or more

Directions

You can do this either on the stove quickly or in the crock pot for later! Here is how to do both!

1. Boil noodles according to package, drain and set aside
2. Chop Velveeta into little cubes
3. Cut butter into square pads

Stovetop:

1. In a large skillet over medium-high heat melt the butter and Velveeta cubes
2. Add milk once it starts getting hot
3. Once that's all melted together add the noodles and mix well

4. Add more milk and butter as needed
5. Serve immediately

Crockpot:

1. In a crockpot add everything together and mix.
2. Set heat to low for 6 hours or high for 3 hours
3. Stir every hour
4. Add more milk and butter if needed

# Cheeseburger Mac

## Ingredients

- 1lb box noodles of choice
- ½ brick of Velveeta cheese
- ½ cup milk or more
- ½ stick of salted butter or more
- 2 pounds of ground beef

## DIRECTIONS

1. In a large skillet or Dutch oven brown ground beef. Drain the grease
2. Add in the butter and cheese to the meat, mix together
3. Add in the milk and simmer for about 10 minutes, so it's all melted together. Stir occasionally

Serve immediately!

# Fried Chicken Bowls

THIS IS ANOTHER ONE of my "Bestie-ipes"! She's got some great ideas too!

Ingredients

- 1/3 bag of popcorn chicken cooked to temperature on the package
- 1 single serve packet dry mashed potato mix
- 1 packet brown gravy
- 1 can whole kernel corn
- 1 cup shredded cheese
- 4 tablespoons butter
- Pinch salt

Directions

1. Make the mashed potatoes according to the package
2. Make the gravy according to its directions
3. Heat the corn in a small saucepan with 4 tablespoons of butter and a pinch of salt
4. In a large bowl or 2 small one's place mashed potatoes on the bottom:
   a. Add popcorn chicken

    b.  Cover with corn
    c.  Cover with gravy
5.  Top with shredded cheese

I changed it a little from how Missy does hers, here's what she does for her family!

"I make loaded mashed potatoes and layer them in a greased 9X13 pan, I add 2 cans of buttered and cooked corn over top. Then I make up 1 package brown gravy and pour that on top. Then I air fry some popcorn chicken until they are done then add that on top add cheese and bake at 350 degrees F or 175 degree C or until cheese is melted, about 15-20 minutes."

Thanks Missy!

# Pepperoni Pinwheels

## INGREDIENTS

- 2 tubes pizza crust
- 1-2 packages pepperoni
- 1 bottle pizza sauce
- 4 cups shredded cheese: 2 cups cheddar 2 cups mozzarella
- ½ stick melted salted butter
- ¼ teaspoon basil

## Directions

1. Preheat oven to 425 degrees F or 220 degrees C, and grease 9X13 pan
2. On a lightly floured countertop, roll out the first pizza dough until you have a nice large rectangle
3. Spread pizza sauce evenly over the dough
4. Layer pepperoni evenly across the sauce leaving a ½ inch edge all the way around.
5. Cover with 1 cup cheddar and 1 cup mozzarella cheese
6. Now we roll. Start from the top and fold over that edge we left, and just keep rolling and tucking the pepperoni

in as you keep rolling and folding towards yourself.

7. Once you've reached the end of the dough leave it seam side down and use either a <u>VERY</u> sharp knife or some form of wire like from a cheese slicer! Cut into 1" rolls like a cinnamon roll!

8. Place into greased pan in rows.

9. Repeat the entire process with the second tube of dough!

10. Once the pinwheels are in place brush the melted butter all over the dough and then sprinkle the basil all over

11. Bake in the oven for 25-30 minutes or until the cheese is nice and bubbly!

# Chili Mac

THIS IS ANOTHER ONE of my Bestie-pies! She makes this one for her family a lot! She says she eats hers with shredded cheese and her husband and one son have sour cream with theirs! YUM!

## INGREDIENTS

- 1 pound ground beef
- 2 tablespoons Cookies Seasoning
- 1 tablespoon Spicy Dan-o's Seasoning (optional)
- 2 tablespoons garlic powder
- 2 tablespoons onion powder
- ¼ cup minced onions
- 1 can chili beans
- 1 can fire roasted tomatoes
- 1 can whole kernel corn
- 2 8-ounce cans of tomato sauce
- 2-pound elbow noodles
- 2 packets chili seasoning (optional)
- 3 ½ cups beef broth

- 5 shakes of *wash-your-sister sauce* Worcestershire sauce

Directions

1. Brown the ground beef in a medium skillet and drain the grease
2. Add in all the seasonings and mix together
3. Drain the first 3 cans; beans, tomatoes, corn, and then add all 4 cans; beans, tomatoes, corn, tomato sauce, to the meat mix then stir to combine
4. Add in the noodles, mix. Add the chili seasoning packets, the broth and Worcestershire sauce
5. Simmer until noodles are done, about 15 minutes
6. Serve with your normal chili fixins'

# Lasagna Stuffed Garlic bread

INGREDIENTS

- 1 tube pizza crust
- 1 pound ground beef
- 1 small jar Prego sauce
- 5 cups shredded cheese
- 1 small tub ricotta cheese
- 4 lasagna noodles
- 4 tablespoons melted butter
- 2 teaspoons oregano

Directions

1. Preheat oven to 425 degrees F or 220 degrees C
2. Brown ground beef. Drain the grease, set aside
3. Roll out pizza crust and drape over edges of a greased cookie sheet
4. Brush with some of the melted butter then sprinkle 1 teaspoon oregano
5. Build your layers:
   a. Meat lengthwise
   b. 2 cups cheese lengthwise

    c.  2 noodles lengthwise
    d.  Ricotta cheese lengthwise
    e.  Meat lengthwise
    f.  2 cups cheese lengthwise
    g.  2 noodles lengthwise
    h.  1 cup shredded cheese lengthwise

6. Start folding edges to the middle:
    a.  take the edge in front of you and pull it up to the middle
    b.  take the right side and pull it to the middle
    c.  take the left side and pull it to the middle
    d.  and take the far edge and pull that up and over the middle
    e.  pinch all the seams you can

7. Brush top with the rest of the butter and sprinkle the rest of the oregano and cheese on top
8. Bake for 12-15 minutes or till the top is golden brown

# Pizza Lovers Bake

INGREDIENTS

- ½ pound noodle of choice! (use elbows, rigatoni, farfalle, bowtie... any of them!)
- 1-pound Italian sausage
- 1 pound ground beef
- 2 jars of pizza sauce, we use the Contadina 15-ounce squeeze bottles, but you can use whatever your family likes best!
- 1 package pepperoni
- 4 cups shredded cheese

Directions

1. Preheat the oven to 350 degrees F or 175 degrees C
2. Cook your noodles according to the package directions
3. In a large skillet brown the ground beef and sausage. Drain the grease
4. Add in the pizza sauces and mix together
5. Drain the noodles and add them to the meat mixture and mix completely

6.  Spread half the meat mixture in the bottom of the 9x13 baking dish
7.  Make one even layer of the pepperoni and cover with 2 cups cheese
8.  Spread the last of the meat mixture on top
9.  If you have any pepperonis left spread them on top
10.  Cover with the last 2 cups of cheese
11.  Bake uncovered for 20-25 minutes, or until cheese is melted and bubbly

# SIDE DISHES

# Cornbread Casserole

INGREDIENTS

- 1 can cream style corn
- 1 can whole kernel corn, drained
- 2 eggs
- 1 box Jiffy mix
- ¼ cup salted butter, melted
- 1 cup sour cream
- 1 cup shredded cheddar cheese

Directions

1. Preheat oven to 350 degrees or 175 degrees C
2. In a large mixing bowl, mix everything together
3. Pour into a greased 9x13 pan
4. Bake for 40-45 minutes or until golden brown

# Green Bean Casserole

INGREDIENTS

- 1 can cream of mushroom soup
- ½ cup of milk
- 2 teaspoons soy sauce
- 1 dash pepper
- 2 cans of any green beans, mainly French cut
- 3 cups French's fried onions split 2:1

Directions

1. Preheat oven to 350 degrees or 175 degrees C. Spray a 9x13 pan
2. In a large bowl, mix everything but the fried onions
3. Add in 2 cups fried onion
4. Pour into greased pan
5. Bake for 25 minutes or until bubbly then stir the bean mix
6. Sprinkle the last cup of onions on top
7. Bake an additional 5-10 minutes, or until golden brown

# Sweet Potato Casserole

INGREDIENTS

- 5 cups cooked and mashed sweet potatoes (real or canned)
- ½ cup (1 stick) melted butter
- 1/3 cup milk
- 1 cup white sugar
- ½ teaspoon vanilla
- 2 eggs, beaten

Topping:

- 1 cup brown sugar
- ½ cup flour
- 1/3 cup softened butter
- 1 cup chopped pecans

Directions

1. Preheat oven to 350 degrees F (175 degrees C) and grease a 9x13 pan
2. In a large bowl mix together mashed potatoes ½ cup

butter, milk, sugar, vanilla, and eggs lightly so there are still chunks of potatoes

3.  Pour into greased pan and set aside
4.  Meanwhile, in a medium bowl combine brown sugar and flour for the topping
5.  Cut in butter until crumbly then fold in pecans.
6.  Sprinkle over sweet potato mix
7.  Bake for 30 minutes or until golden brown

# At Home Fiesta Potatoes

INGREDIENTS

- 2 pounds of russet potatoes
- 1 cup all-purpose flour
- ½ teaspoon onion powder
- ½ teaspoon garlic powder
- ¼ teaspoon paprika
- ¼ teaspoon cayenne pepper
- 1 can Rico's liquid cheese
- Sour cream

Directions

1. Wash and peel potatoes, then cut into cubes, rinse, and pat dry on a paper towel
2. Heat oil in a deep fryer to 350 degrees or 175 degrees C
3. Combine all the dry ingredients in a medium sized bowl
4. In medium batches, drop the cubes into the flour and coat well
5. Shake off any of the excess flour before dropping into

the fryer

6. Let fry for about 12 minutes
7. Remove from grease and let dry on a wire rack on a cookie sheet
8. Heat liquid cheese according to the can's directions
9. Serve with sour cream and chives if desired

# Midwest Party Potatoes

INGREDIENTS

- 1 can cream of chicken soup
- 1 cup sour cream
- ¼ cup melted butter
- 1 cup milk
- Seasonings of choice, I use:
    - 2 tablespoons garlic powder
    - 2 tablespoons onion powder
    - 1 tablespoon salt
    - 1 tablespoon pepper
- 1 small onion, diced
- 2 cups cheese of choice
- 30 oz package of shredded hashbrowns
- Crunchy layer; your choice!
    - Cheddar and sour cream chips *our favorite! *
    - Ritz crackers
    - Corn flakes
    - Club crackers

Directions

1. Preheat oven to 350 degrees F and grease a 9X13 pan
2. Mix everything except the hashbrowns and the crunchy layer, in a large bowl until blended, adjust seasonings to taste!
3. Gently mix in the hashbrowns till covered. This might be kind of hard since the hashbrowns are frozen!
4. Spread evenly into that greased pan and coat with your crunchy choice!
5. Bake for 1 hour or till its bubbly

# SWEETS AND TREATS

# Fruit Fluff Salad

INGREDIENTS

- 1 3-ounce box Jello of choice, we like: raspberry, cherry, strawberry, orange, ones that are potent flavors
- 1 small 24-ounce tub cottage cheese
- 1 8-ounce tub whipped topping
- 4 bananas
- Up to 4 different cans (15 ounces) of fruit, We like:
    - Mandarin oranges
    - Fruit cocktail
    - Maraschino cherries
    - Pineapple chunks
    - Peaches
    - Pears
    - Apricots
- ½ small bag of mini marshmallows

Directions

1. Empty cottage cheese into a medium size bowl and mix in whipped topping
2. Sprinkle with Jello powder and mix till all one color

3.  Meanwhile, in a strainer in your sink, drain your cans of fruit. Once drained, pour into whipped Jello mix
4.  Cut up all 4 bananas into nice sized coins and pour in the mini marshmallows and fold in gently.
5.  Set in fridge for at least 5 hours to chill or even over night before serving!

# Mandarin Orange Salad

INGREDIENTS

- 1 3-ounce box orange Jello
- 1 24-ounce tub cottage cheese
- 1 8-ounce tub whipped topping
- 1 15-ounce can mandarin oranges
- 1 15-ounce can crushed pineapple
- ½ bag mini marshmallows
- ½ bag coconut (optional)

Directions

1. Mix cottage cheese, whipped topping, and Jello together till all one color
2. Drain the oranges and pineapple and add to the whipped Jello
3. Fold in marshmallows and coconut if desired
4. Place in fridge for 5 hours or overnight before serving

# Cream Cheese Fluff Salad

INGREDIENTS

- 1 8oz cream cheese block
- ¼ cup sugar
- 1 container (12oz) defrosted whipped topping
- 3 bananas cut it to coins
- 1 can crushed pineapple
- 1 can fruit cocktail
- 1 large apple- we like to use a nice big granny smith green apple!
- ½ cup golden raisins
- ½ cup chopped pecans (optional)
- ½ cup chopped coconut (optional)

Directions

1. In a large bowl, with a hand mixer, beat the cream cheese and sugar together until smooth.
2. Add in the whipped topping and beat on high to combine the cream cheese and whipped cream
3. Open all cans and pour into strainer to drain all extra juice

4. Begin adding your fruits of choice. Fold in gently
5. Make sure to chill for at least 2 hours before serving to make sure its set

# Blueberry Blondies

THIS IS SO EASY AND so delicious, and you can really do just about anything instead of blueberries. I've done raspberries, chocolate chip and butterscotch chips, I tried strawberries, but they didn't turn out the best! You can make these in a big 9x13 pan or 2 8x8 square pans!

Ingredients

- ½ cup (1 whole stick) salted butter, softened but not melted!
- 1 cup sugar
- 1 teaspoon vanilla
- 2 large eggs
- 1 cup flour
- ¼ teaspoon baking powder
- ¼ teaspoon salt
- 1 package blueberries or whatever you choose to use! Fresh is the best I've found! But it's up to you!

Instructions

1. Preheat oven to 350 degrees and grease your pan of choice.

2. In a large bowl (I use my stand mixer, it's easier!) cream together the butter and sugar and vanilla until light and fluffy

3. Beat in the eggs one at a time and make sure to scrape the bowl after each egg.

4. SLOWLY add the flour and mix on medium low speed so flour doesn't go everywhere! Once all the flour is added mix until completely blended.

5. Remove from mixer and gently fold in blueberries.

6. Pour in to greased pan and bake for 35-40 minutes or until you can see the edges pull away from your pan and it looks golden brown. (the outside temperature does have influence if it's too hot outside its going to take longer to bake. Don't ask me why, just trust me! And if it's colder out it might only take 25-30 min to be golden!)

7. Make sure to let this cool on a wire rack in the pan before you lift it out of the pan.

# French Silk Pie

YOU CAN EITHER MAKE this all or if you want a quick short cut, you can use a store-bought Oreo cookie crust. Just remember though, you WILL have some of that delicious mix left over so you might want to have 2 crusts! You are also going to need a stand mixer **and** hand mixer or 2 of each. Trust me, it's easier!

Ingredients for the crust:

- 20 Oreos (I used the double stuffed ones!!)
- 4 tablespoons melted salted butter

For the Filling:

- 1 1/3 cup sugar
- 4 large eggs
- 8 oz melted baking chocolate, I use milk chocolate because I'm not a major fan of dark chocolate, but you can do whatever works best for you!
- 4 teaspoons vanilla extract, split 2 and 2
- 10 tablespoons butter at room temperature, that's 1 whole stick plus 2 tablespoons from another stick! I cut mine into cubes so it's easier to rise to room

temperature!
- 1 1/3 cups heavy cream
- 4 teaspoons powdered sugar

For the topping

- 1 cup heavy cream
- 2 tablespoons powdered sugar
- 1 teaspoon vanilla extract
- Chocolate shavings or coco powder, I get a Bakers chocolate bar and use my veggie peeler to shave some nice curls and that's my topping!

## DIRECTIONS
**Make the crust:**

1. Preheat the oven to 350 F or 175 degrees C and spray at least one 9-inch pie dish
2. Place Oreo cookies into either a food processer or in a gallon bag. Pulse the food processor till finely chopped or put in a gallon bag and beat with a rolling pin until nice and fine!
3. Pour into a bowl and add in the melted butter and mix till moist.
4. Pour the crust into the pie dish and pat flat into the corners and up the sides of the dish, bake for 10 minutes or till fragrant then let cool on a wire rack

**Make the filling:**

1.  In a small saucepan melt and whisk together the sugar and the eggs over medium-low, stirring constantly. At the same time melt the baking chocolate in either a double boiler or in 30 second increments in the microwave.
2.  Once the sugar mix is heated to 160 F and covers the back of a metal spoon, remove from the heat. Mix in the melted chocolate and 2 tsp vanilla. Stir till blended, then cool till just warm
3.  With an electric mixer beat the butter till light and fluffy, about 2 to 3 minutes.
4.  Gradually add in the cooled chocolate mixture then beat on high for 5 minutes. DO NOT SKIP OR SHORTEN!!!!!
5.  In another medium bowl using your other mixer, beat the cream until it begins to thicken, then add in the powder sugar and the vanilla and beat until stiff peaks form, another 5 minutes. DO NOT SHORTEN!!!
6.  Then fold into the cooled chocolate mixture into the whipped topping. If the chocolate is still HOT do NOT mix it together, it will undo all your hard work. Do not over mix either, that turns it soupy fast too!
7.  Once nicely folded in pour your chocolate mix SLOWLY into the pie dish it will either be very tall, or you can go ahead and make yourself a mini pie with what's left! Chill for at least 6 hours. Or overnight. At this point this pie can sit in the fridge for 2 days ahead of time.

**Make the topping:**

- Using an electric mixer to beat the heavy cream, powdered sugar, and vanilla on high speed until stiff peaks form. Top pie with the whipped cream and sprinkle your coco powder or chocolate shavings on top!

# Butterbeer Pie

FOR THE PIE:

- 2 premade pie crusts
- 1 ½ cups heavy cream
- 2 teaspoon vanilla
- 1 tablespoon powder sugar
- 1 package instant butterscotch pudding mix
- 1 ½ cups cold milk
- ¼ cup caramel (I just use the good ice cream topping kind!)

For the marshmallow whipped cream

- 1 cup heavy cream
- 2 teaspoon vanilla
- 1 tablespoon powder sugar
- ½ cup marshmallow fluff
- Gold sprinkles

Directions

1. Preheat the oven to 350 degrees F or 175 degrees C

and line a cookie sheet with either parchment paper or silicone sheet.

2. Roll out pie crust out and drape over a 9-inch pie dish, fit crust to dish and crimp the edges, prick the bottom with a fork and bake till lightly golden brown about 18 minutes. You may want to fill with pie weights because my sides always shrink.

3. Meanwhile, if you stick with the Harry Potter theme, cut out a nice sized lightning bolt. Otherwise find your favorite shape and cut out that shape and set on another lined baking sheet. (I've got some pretty crazy ones, I've made a buffalo, a watering can, a dachshund, and a dachshund from behind, I even free handed a snitch in flight and the Hogwarts house shield!

4. Bake your designs for no more than 10 minutes

5. Make sure to let both crust and toppers cool to room temp

6. Meanwhile, in a large bowl using a hand mixer, beat the heavy cream, vanilla, and powder sugar on high for about 6 minutes or till soft peaks form.

7. In another large bowl mix the pudding and milk according to package then let stand until thick.

8. Once pudding is thickened, fold in the caramel and whipped cream until combined.

9. SLOWLY pour pudding mix into pie dish, be careful, you might have leftovers.

10. Make sure to chill for at least 3 hours, or even overnight.

11. To make the marshmallow whipped topping; in a large bowl, using a hand mixer add the heavy cream, vanilla

and powdered sugar and beat till stiff peaks form which is about 6 minutes. Then slowly fold in marshmallow fluff. It's going to be sticky and tough so it may take a few minutes.

12. Spread whipped topping all over pie and then place your cut out lightning bolt or whatever shape you chose on top! Cover with as many sprinkles as you like. I also went out and found some edible gold powder that I also sprinkled on top with my sprinkles!

# Jolly Good Cookies

THIS IS THE BEST BASE recipe for any kind of cookie you want to make. I use chocolate chips, butterscotch chips, white chocolate chips, Reese's chips, and M&M's! Use your imagination for what kind of cookies you want!

Ingredients

- 1 stick of salted butter softened
- ¾ cup sugar
- ¾ cup brown sugar
- 1 teaspoon vanilla extract
- 2 eggs at room temperature
- 2 1/3 cups flour
- 1 teaspoon salt
- 1 teaspoon baking soda
- 3 cups of your chips, candy, or filling of choice

Directions

1. Preheat the oven to 350 degrees F or 175 degrees C
2. In a medium bowl combine flour, salt and baking soda and then set aside
3. In another medium bowl using an electric mixer, beat

butter, both sugars and vanilla until creamy

4. Add eggs, one at a time, mixing well after each egg is added
5. Slowly add the flour into the mixture until blended
6. Fold in your filling gently
7. Using a cookie scoop or two regular spoons, make balls no bigger than 2 inches and plop them on to a baking sheet either lined with parchment paper, silicone mat, or sprayed with cooking spray. Give them enough room to spread, so if you have a 9x13 sheet I wouldn't do more than 12 on your tray
8. Bake for 10 minutes and make sure the cookies don't brown
9. Remove and let them cool on the pan for 5 minutes and then set them on a wire cooling rack to finish cooling

***This recipe makes about 3 dozen if you make the scoops small enough! ***

# Scotch-a-roos

FROM WHAT I KNOW THESE are another Midwest dessert that can either be really good or too much! I would like to think that these have found that happy middle!

INGREDIENTS

- 1 cup light corn syrup (the clear stuff!)
- 1 cup sugar
- 1 ½ cups JIFF peanut butter (this time brand matters!!)
- 6 cups crispy rice cereal
- 1 cup chocolate chips
- 1 cup butterscotch chips

Directions

1. Generously spray a 9x13 baking dish and then set aside
2. In a large stock pot mix together the corn syrup, sugar, and peanut butter. Cook over medium heat stirring until peanut butter melts and everything blends

together

3. Bring to a boil and then remove from heat and add in crispy rice

4. Once mixed transfer to the greased dish, spray your hands so they don't stick and pat mix into the pan and make it nice and even, set aside

5. In a medium saucepan over medium low heat, melt both baking chips until smooth then spread over the bars and let everything cool!

# Jolly Good Punkin' Pie

## INGREDIENTS

- 1 9-inch unbaked pie crust
- 2 eggs
- 1 16 ounce can pumpkin pie puree
- 1 14 ounce can sweetened condensed milk
- 1 ½ teaspoon pumpkin pie spice

## Directions

1. Preheat the oven to 425 degrees F 220 degrees C
2. In a large bowl combine eggs, puree, milk, and spice. Mix until combined
3. Lay pie crust over 9-inch greased pie dish and stretch and tuck into the corners
4. Pour pumpkin mix into crust
5. Place pie dish on a baking sheet and bake at 425 degrees F for 15 minutes, then reduce the heat to 350 degrees F and continue baking till filling is set, about 35-40 minutes
6. Serve with whipped topping or vanilla ice cream

# Punkin' Fluff Dip

INGREDIENTS

- 1 16-ounce thawed container of whipped topping
- 1 5-ounce package of instant vanilla pudding
- 1 15-ounce can solid pack pumpkin
- 1 teaspoon pumpkin pie spice

Directions

1. In a large bowl mix together the pudding and the pumpkin and pie spice until smooth
2. Fold in the thawed whipped topping and mix till blended again
3. Chill in the fridge for at least 3 hours prior to serving

# **About the Author**

From a small town in the Northesat corner of Iowa, I learned how to cook from my Grandma before she passed away, watching things on Facebook and YouTube and from just watching my mom and dad growing up. I love to eat and everything that I make tastes so much better because ***I made that!!!!*** Everything in this is something I have made for my family so we know they are all winners! I hope your family loves them like mine does!

Don't be afraid to tweak these to your fmailies tastes also! Thats how most of my recipies have started!

Read more at https://www.instagram.com/ katelynkhaos08/.

www.ingramcontent.com/pod-product-compliance
Lightning Source LLC
Chambersburg PA
CBHW070549160726
48003CB00005B/1970